THE DASH DIET
COOKBOOK

The DASH Diet Cookbook

Quick and Easy DASH Diet Recipes for Health and Weight Loss

DYLANNA**PRESS**

CONTENTS

INTRODUCTION

The DASH diet is one of the most researched and well-respected diets available today. It is not a fad diet or a quick weight-loss scheme, but instead a guide to a healthier way of eating and living.

The DASH diet was developed to lower blood pressure, one of the leading factors in heart disease. In addition to lowering blood pressure, the diet has been found to be more nutritious and lead to better health in all areas when compared with the standard American diet (SAD).

This book was designed to make following the DASH diet simple, easy, and most importantly great tasting. Included is an overview of the DASH diet covering the foods and portions to eat on the diet, a grocery list to help you stock your kitchen, sample eating plans, and more than 50 delicious recipes for breakfast, lunch, dinner, and dessert.

Read on to get started with the DASH diet and be on your way to better health!

Overview of the DASH Diet

The DASH diet was recently named the best and healthiest diet by nutrition experts at US News and World Report.[*] This was the fifth year in a row that the DASH diet took top honors.

DASH stands for Dietary Approaches to Stop Hypertension and it is designed as a life-long approach to treating or preventing hypertension (high blood pressure). It is often prescribed by doctors as a first step in dealing with pre-hypertension as a way of avoiding blood pressure medications.

The DASH diet focuses on reducing the amount of sodium in your diet and increasing nutrient-rich foods such as fruits, vegetables, and whole grains. Research has shown that by following the DASH diet you can reduce your blood

---

[*]   http://health.usnews.com/best-diet

pressure by as much as 12 points, which is as effective as taking a medication.[**] In addition to helping to lower blood pressure, the DASH diet has many other health benefits. These include:

- decreased risk of heart disease
- decreased risk of cancer
- decreased risk of diabetes
- decreased risk of stroke
- lower cholesterol levels
- helps to prevent osteoporosis
- helps to promote weight loss

For these reasons, the DASH diet is a smart choice for anyone looking to improve their health.

Daily Nutrient Goals for the DASH Diet

Below are the daily nutrient guidelines set by the National Heart, Lung, and Blood Institute:[***]

Daily Nutrient Goals for the DASH Diet

Total fat: 27% of calories
Saturated fat: 6% of calories
Protein: 18% of calories
Carbohydrate: 55% of calories
Cholesterol: 150 mg
Sodium: 2,300 mg/1,500 mg*
Potassium: 4,700 mg
Calcium: 1,250 mg
Magnesium: 500 mg
Fiber: 30 g

* 1,500 mg sodium has been found to be even better for lowering blood pressure. It was particularly effective for middle-aged and older individuals, African Americans, and those who already had high blood pressure. g = grams; mg = milligrams

---

[**]   http://www.health.harvard.edu/press_releases/diet-can-lower-blood-pressure-as-much-as-taking-a-medication
[***]   http://www.nhlbi.nih.gov/health/resources/heart/hbp-dash-how-plan-html

It is recommended that you consult with your doctor to determine whether you should follow the 2,300 or 1,500 mg sodium recommendations.

DASH Diet Eating Plan

The DASH diet eating plan focuses on including fresh fruits and vegetables, low-fat dairy products, and lean sources of protein into your daily diet. It aims to reduce the amount of salt and sodium, added sugar, fats, and red meat. The diet is rich in nutrients that promote low blood pressure including potassium, magnesium, calcium, protein, and fiber. Below are the recommendations for daily servings based on a 2,000 calorie per day diet. These guidelines were developed by the National Institutes of Health.

Whole grains: 6 to 8 servings per day

This category includes breads, pasta, oats, cereals, rice, quinoa, rye as well as other grains. It is recommended that you choose whole grains over white and refined grains.

Sample servings:

- 1 slice bread
- 1 ounce cereal
- ½ cup cooked pasta or rice

Vegetables: 4 to 6 servings per day

This category includes asparagus, broccoli, Brussels sprouts, carrots, celery, green beans, green leafy vegetables, kale, lettuce, peppers, potatoes, pumpkin, spinach, squash, sweet potatoes, tomatoes, and turnips as well as other vegetables.

Sample servings:

- 1 cup leafy greens
- ½ cup cooked or raw vegetables
- ½ cup vegetable juice

Fruits: 4 to 6 servings per day

This category includes apples, bananas, cherries, dates, grapes, grapefruit, lemons, mangoes, melons, peaches, pears, pineapple, raisins, strawberries, and watermelon as well as other fruits.

Sample servings:

- 1 medium apple, peach, or pear
- ½ cup fresh, frozen, or canned fruit
- ¼ dried fruit

Dairy products: 2 to 3 servings per day

This category includes low-fat/nonfat milk, buttermilk, low-fat/nonfat cheeses, and low-fat/nonfat yogurt.

Sample servings:

- 1 cup (8 ounces) milk or yogurt
- 1 ½ ounces cheese

Lean protein: 3 to 6 servings per day

This category includes meats, poultry, fish, and eggs. Choose lean cuts of meat and trim away excess fat. Remove skin from poultry.

Sample servings:

- 1 egg
- 1 ounce cooked meat (to visualize, 4 ounces is about the size of a deck of cards)

Nuts, seeds, legumes: 3 to 5 servings per week

This category includes almonds, black beans, hazelnuts, kidney beans, legumes, lentils, peanuts, pumpkin seeds, split peas, and sunflower seeds as well other nuts, seeds, and legumes.

Sample servings:
- 1/3 cup (1 ½ ounces) nuts
- 2 tablespoons peanut butter
- 2 tablespoons sunflower seeds
- ½ cup cooked legumes

Fats and oils: 2-3 serving per day

This category includes coconut oil, ghee, low-fat mayonnaise, margarine, olive oil, salad dressings, and vegetable oils.

Sample servings:

- 1 teaspoon olive oil
- 1 teaspoon margarine
- 1 tablespoons mayonnaise
- 2 tablespoons salad dressing

Sweets and sugars: 5 or less per week

This category includes fruit-flavored gelatin, candy, jelly, maple syrup, sorbet, and sugar.

Sample servings:

- 1 tablespoon sugar
- 1 tablespoon jam
- ½ cup sorbet

The following table outlines the number of recommended daily servings for various calorie levels. The amount of calories needed per day depends on a number of factors including your current age, weight, gender, and activity level.

DASH Eating Plan—Number of Daily Servings for Other Calorie Levels

Servings/Day

Food Groups	1,600 calories/day	2,600 calories/day	3,100 calories/day
Grains	6	10-11	12-13
Vegetables	3-4	5-6	6
Fruits	4	5-6	6
Nonfat or lowfat dairy products	2-3	3	3-4
Lean meats, poultry, and fish	3-6	6	6-9
Nuts, seeds, and legumes	3/week	1	1
Fats and oils	2	3	4
Sweets and sugars	0	less than 2	less than 2

Spices and Seasonings

If you are used to seasoning your food with salt, then doing without may take some getting used to it. But rest assured that there are many alternative ways to amp up the flavor of your food without resorting to shaking salt on it. As an added benefit, many herbs and spices contain powerful antioxidants and other properties that are highly beneficial to your health. Below is a list of herbs and spices that can be used to replace salt on the DASH diet to add flavor to your food.

- **Basil:** Basil is one of the most common herbs used in cooking. It has a slightly sweet and pungent taste.
- **Bay leaves:** These sweet and aromatic leaves are often used to enhance the flavor of meats, stews, and other dishes.
- **Cardamom:** Cardamom is a popular spice in Indian cooking with a peppery and citrusy taste.
- **Cayenne:** Cayenne has a hot and peppery flavor that will definitely spice up a dish. Also called red chili pepper.
- **Cinnamon:** Cinnamon can help to regulate blood sugar and

lower cholesterol.
- **Garlic/garlic powder**: Garlic, whether fresh or in powder form, is a great alternative to salt as it not only enhances taste but has many known health-boosting properties.
- **Ginger:** Ginger can be used either fresh or as a powder and in addition to adding flavor has many health benefits.
- **Lemon juice:** A squeeze of lemon juice adds a fresh citrusy flavor that can enhance the flavor of many foods.
- **Onion powder:** Onion powder has a strong taste that many people love, but use sparingly or its flavor can overpower a dish.
- **Pepper (black):** You may think of salt and pepper as a dynamic duo but pepper is perfectly capable of standing alone. It will enhance the flavor of any dish. Choose freshly ground black pepper for a more distinct and intense taste.

Top Hidden Sources of Sodium

You may think that just passing on the salt shaker will be enough to lower the amount of sodium in your diet. However, you might be surprised to learn about the many products that contain hidden sodium. Here are some of the top culprits.

SODIUM IN COMMON FOODS

Bread and baked goods: Bread is one of the top sources of dietary sodium. One slice of bread can contain anywhere from 350-700 milligrams of sodium. Read labels carefully and choose a brand with the lowest sodium content. Other baked goods such as doughnuts, muffins, and cakes made from baking mixes are also loaded with sodium.

Breakfast cereals: The amount of salt in cereals varies widely so it is important to read labels carefully.

Condiments and sauces: The majority of store-bought condiments such as ketchup, mustard, salad dressings, soy sauce, relish, barbecue sauce, and jarred spaghetti sauce are loaded with sodium. Read labels carefully and buy reduced or no-sodium products whenever possible. Even better, make your own homemade sauces and dressings.

Cheese and dairy products: Most people don't think of salt when it comes to cheese, but salt is used in the cheese-making process and they are a significant source of sodium in the diet. Milk also contains sodium, 120 milligrams per half-cup serving.

Canned foods: Salt is used to flavor and preserve most canned foods such as soups, stews, and vegetables. A can of Campbell's chicken noodle soup has a whopping 900 milligrams of sodium per serving. Canned beans are also high in sodium content. Look for low-salt and salt-free versions or make your own.

STOCKING YOUR KITCHEN

A big part of preparing meals without a lot of fuss is having the ingredients you need on hand. Keeping your pantry stocked with a few essentials will go a long way toward making it easy to prepare a quick and healthy DASH diet meal.

Cleaning Out

If you're committed to incorporating the DASH diet principles into your eating, the first thing you need to do is clean out your refrigerator, freezer, and pantry. Look carefully at all of the labels of everything in your kitchen. Get rid of anything that is high in sodium, sugar, white flour, or saturated and trans fats.

Restocking

Now that you've gotten rid of all the foods that may be causing problems, it's time to stock up on a few basics to keep on hand.

Pantry Items

- 100% whole-wheat bread (small slice) and pita pockets
- Applesauce, unsweetened
- Baking powder and baking soda
- Beans (dried and/or canned)
- Brown rice
- Brown sugar

- Chicken, beef and/or vegetable broth, low-sodium
- Cornstarch or arrowroot
- Dried fruit and nuts
- Flour (unbleached and whole wheat)
- Granola bars, low-fat
- Marinade, low-sodium – try the Mrs. Dash brand
- Oatmeal (whole oats or quick cooking, not instant)
- Olive and canola oils
- Pretzels (unsalted)
- Quinoa
- Reduced-sodium ketchup, deli mustard, "lite" mayonnaise
- Salad dressings, low-sodium, a good brand to try is Consorzio
- Salsa
- Tomato sauce, low-sodium
- Tomatoes, canned, no-salt-added
- Tuna packed in water
- Vegetable oil spray
- Vinegar (balsamic and white wine)
- Whole-grain cereals (shredded wheat, toasted oat, bran flakes)
- Whole-wheat pasta
- Whole-wheat snack crackers, low-sodium

Refrigerator Items

- Bottled lemon juice
- Eggs and/or egg substitute
- Fresh fruit
- Fresh vegetables
- Fresh-pack salad greens
- Garlic
- Lemons
- Lime
- Low-fat and nonfat yogurt
- Low-fat cottage cheese
- Low-fat or nonfat milk
- Natural peanut butter
- Onions
- Reduced-fat string cheese
- Reduced-fat, low-sodium deli meat
- Reduced-sodium soy sauce and teriyaki sauce
- Tortillas, whole wheat or corn

- Trans-fat-free margarine

Freezer Items
- Fish
- Frozen fruit (without added sugar)
- Frozen vegetables (no sauces or salt)
- Homemade soups and broth – freeze in single servings
- Lean meats
- Low-calorie frozen desserts

Recipes

BREAKFAST

Apple-Cinnamon Baked Oatmeal

This oatmeal recipe is cooked in the slow cooker so you can wake up to a warm and satisfying breakfast without any fuss.

Servings: 8

Ingredients:

- 2 cups steel cut oats
- 8 cups water
- 1 tsp cinnamon
- 1/2 tsp allspice
- 1/2 tsp nutmeg
- 1/4 cup brown sugar
- 1 tsp vanilla extract
- 2 apples, diced
- 1 cup raisins
- 1/2 cup unsalted, roasted walnuts, chopped

Directions:

1. Spray slow cooker with nonstick cooking spray.
2. Add all ingredients to slow cooker except for walnuts. Mix well to combine.
3. Set slow cooker to low setting and cook for 8 hours.
4. Serve topped with chopped walnuts

Nutritional Information (per serving)

- Calories: 312
- Sodium: 4 mg
- Protein: 9 g
- Carbs: 60 g
- Fat: 7.5 g

Note: Be sure to use steel cut oats for this recipe (not instant or rolled oats) or you may end up with a sticky mess.

Egg White Vegetable Omelet

An omelet makes a perfect breakfast, lunch, or even dinner on the DASH diet. You can use whatever vegetables you have on hand and in just a few minutes be eating a healthy, high-protein meal.

Servings: 2

Ingredients:

- 6 egg whites
- 1 tablespoon water
- 2 teaspoon olive oil
- ½ yellow onion, chopped
- 1 tomato, diced
- 2-3 asparagus stalks, cut into small pieces
- 3-4 mushrooms, sliced

Directions:

1   Whisk egg whites in a medium bowl, add tablespoon of water, and whisk with fork until well blended.

2   Heat 1 teaspoon oil over medium-high heat in a medium size skillet. Add onion, tomato, asparagus, and mushrooms and sauté until vegetables are tender, about 3-4 minutes. Remove from pan and set aside.

3   Add another teaspoon of oil to the pan and allow to heat for a minute or two. Add beaten eggs to pan, tilting pan as needed so eggs cover entire pan. Let eggs set along edges of pan, this should only take a few seconds if pan is hot enough. Using spatula slide eggs away from sides of pan and tilt pan to allow more egg mixture to flow to pan surface. Repeat until eggs are almost finished, but still soft in the middle.

4   Add vegetable mixture to middle of omelet. Fold one side of omelet over toppings. Slide onto plate. Voila, it is ready to eat.

Nutritional Information (per serving)
- Calories: 145
- Sodium: 77 mg
- Protein: 8.5 g
- Carbs: 19 g
- Fat: 4.5 g

Fruity Green Smoothie

This vitamin-packed smoothie is an antioxidant powerhouse, packing 2 ½ servings of fruits and veggies in each serving.

Servings: 1

Ingredients:

- 2 cups fresh spinach leaves
- 1 medium banana, peeled
- 7-8 strawberries, trimmed
- ½ cup orange juice
- 1 cup crushed ice

Directions:

1. Place all ingredients into a blender and blend until smooth.
2. Serve in tall glass.

Nutritional Information (per serving)

- Calories: 235
- Sodium: 64 mg
- Protein: 5 g
- Carbs: 56 g
- Fat: 1.5 g

Fruit and Yogurt Breakfast Salad

The whole grains in this breakfast salad will keep you full and energized through lunch.

Servings: 6

Ingredients:

- 2 cups water
- 1/4 teaspoon salt
- 3/4 cup quick cooking brown rice
- 3/4 cup bulgur
- 1 large apple, cored and chopped
- 1 large pear, cored and chopped
- 1 orange, peeled and cut into sections
- 1 cup dried cranberries
- 1 container (8 ounces) low-fat or nonfat Greek style yogurt, plain

Directions:

1. Heat water in a large pot over high heat until boiling.
2. Add in salt, rice, and bulgur. Reduce heat to low, cover, and simmer for 10 minutes. Remove from heat and let sit covered for 2 minutes.
3. Transfer grains to large bowl and refrigerate until chilled.
4. Remove chilled grains from refrigerator. Add apple, pear, oranges, and dried cranberries. Fold in yogurt and mix gently until grains and fruit are thoroughly coated.
5. Serve in bowls.

Note: Grains can be prepared the night before and chilled overnight in the refrigerator.

Nutritional Information (per serving)
- Calories: 190
- Sodium: 118 mg
- Protein: 4 g
- Carbs: 40 g
- Fat: 1 g

Blueberry Breakfast Quinoa

Quinoa makes an excellent gluten-free alternative to oatmeal.

Servings: 4

Ingredients:

- 2 cups low-fat/nonfat milk
- 1 cup quinoa, uncooked
- 1/4 cup honey
- 1/2 teaspoon cinnamon
- 1/4 cup chopped almonds, pecans, or walnuts
- 1/2 cup fresh blueberries

Directions:

1   In a saucepan, bring milk to a low boil. Add quinoa and return to boil. Cover, reduce heat to low, and simmer until most of liquid is absorbed, about 12-15 minutes. Remove from heat.

2   Stir remaining ingredients into quinoa, cover, and allow to stand for an additional 10 minutes before serving.

Note: For a thinner consistency, add more milk.

Nutritional Information (per serving)
• Calories: 320
• Sodium: 70 mg
• Protein: 12 g
• Carbs: 59 g
• Fat: 5 g

Healthy Low-Fat Granola

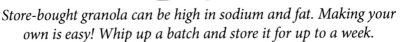

Store-bought granola can be high in sodium and fat. Making your own is easy! Whip up a batch and store it for up to a week.

Servings: 8

Ingredients:

- 4 cups old-fashioned oats
- 1/4 cup flax seed
- 1/4 cup wheat germ
- 1/4 cup coconut flakes
- 1/4 cup pumpkin or sunflower seeds
- 1/4 sliced almonds
- 1/3 cup maple syrup
- 1/4 cup apple juice
- 1 teaspoon cinnamon
- 1 teaspoon vanilla
- 1/4 teaspoon salt

Directions:

1. Preheat oven to 325 degrees F.
2. In a large bowl, combine all ingredients. Stir well to thoroughly coat all ingredients.
3. Line rimmed cookie sheet with parchment paper. Spread mixture evenly on cookie sheet.
4. Bake in oven for 30-35 minutes, stirring once, until lightly browned.

Nutritional Information (per serving)
- Calories: 180
- Sodium: 85 mg
- Protein: 5 g
- Carbs: 30.5 g
- Fat: 5.2 g

Greek-Style Breakfast Scramble

Feta cheese and spinach team up in this healthy, protein-packed breakfast.

Servings: 1

Ingredients:

- Nonstick cooking spray
- 1 cup fresh spinach, chopped
- 1/2 cup mushrooms, chopped
- 1/4 onion, chopped
- 1 whole egg and 2 egg whites
- 2 tablespoons feta cheese
- Freshly ground black pepper, to taste

Directions:

1. Heat a nonstick skillet over medium heat. Spray with cooking spray and add spinach, mushrooms, and onion. Sauté for 2-3 minutes until onions turn translucent and spinach has wilted.
2. Meanwhile, whisk egg and egg whites together in a bowl. Add feta cheese and pepper.
3. Pour egg mixture over vegetables. Cook eggs, stirring with spatula, for 3-4 minutes, or until eggs are cooked through.
4. Serve hot.

Nutritional Information (per serving)
- Calories: 150
- Sodium: 440 mg
- Protein: 17 g
- Carbs: 6 g
- Fat: 7 g

Lemon-Zucchini Muffins

These muffins are a great way to sneak in an extra serving of vegetables.

Servings: 12 muffins

Ingredients:
- 2 cups all-purpose flour
- 1/2 cup sugar
- 1 tablespoon baking powder
- 1/4 teaspoon salt
- 1/4 teaspoon cinnamon
- 1/4 teaspoon nutmeg
- 1 cup shredded zucchini
- 3/4 cup nonfat milk
- 2 tablespoons olive oil
- 2 tablespoons lemon juice
- 1 egg
- Nonstick cooking spray

Directions:
1. Preheat oven to 400 degrees F. Prepare muffin tin by spraying lightly with cooking spray or lining with muffin liners.
2. In a mixing bowl, combine flour, sugar, baking powder, salt, cinnamon, and nutmeg.
3. In a separate bowl, combine zucchini, milk, oil, lemon juice, and egg. Stir well.
4. Add zucchini mixture to flour mixture. Stir until just combined. Do not over stir.
5. Pour batter into prepared muffin cups. Bake for 20 minutes or until light golden brown.

Nutritional Information (per serving)
- Calories: 145
- Sodium: 62 mg
- Protein: 3 g
- Carbs: 25 g
- Fat: 4 g

Spiced Pumpkin Pancakes

Whole-wheat flour makes these hearty pancakes extra nutritious.

Servings: 10 (2 pancakes per serving)

Ingredients:

- 2 cups whole wheat flour
- 2 teaspoons baking powder
- 1 teaspoon baking soda
- 1 teaspoon cinnamon
- 1/2 teaspoon ground nutmeg
- 1/2 teaspoon ground ginger
- 1/4 cup brown sugar
- 1 egg yolk
- 1 cup canned pumpkin
- 2 tablespoons coconut oil
- 2 cups skim milk
- 2 egg whites

Directions:

1. In a mixing bowl, combine together flour, baking powder, baking soda, cinnamon, nutmeg, and ginger.
2. In another bowl, mix together brown sugar, egg yolk, pumpkin, and coconut oil. Stir in milk.
3. Pour milk mixture into bowl with dry ingredients and stir until just combined. Do not over stir.
4. Beat egg whites in a bowl until fluffy. Fold egg whites into pancake batter.
5. Heat a nonstick griddle or large skillet over medium high heat. Spray with nonstick cooking spray.
6. When griddle is hot, ladle batter by 1/4 cup amounts onto pan. Cook until batter starts to bubble, flip, and cook until lightly browned.

Nutritional Information (per serving)
- Calories: 150
- Sodium: 360 mg
- Protein: 6.6 g
- Carbs: 32 g
- Fat: 2 g

Blueberry-Maple Refrigerator Oatmeal

Refrigerator oatmeal is so simple to make and so yummy to eat.

Servings: 1

Ingredients:

- 1/2 cup rolled oats (old-fashioned style, not instant)
- 1/2 cup water or nonfat milk
- Pinch of sea salt
- 1 tablespoon chia seeds (optional)
- 1-2 teaspoons maple syrup
- 2 cups fresh blueberries

Directions:

1. In a bowl or jar, combine oats, water or milk, and salt. Cover and place in refrigerator overnight.
2. Before serving, top with chia seeds, maple syrup, and blueberries.

Nutritional Information (per serving)
- Calories: 260
- Sodium: 160 mg
- Protein: 9 g
- Carbs: 49 g
- Fat: 4 g

SOUPS AND SALADS

Potato-Leek Soup

Another great-tasting soup, easily prepared in under 30 minutes.
Freeze in single-serving freezer bags and reheat for
an almost-instant meal.

Servings: 8

Ingredients:

- 2 tablespoons olive oil
- 3 leeks, washed and sliced
- 1 teaspoon thyme
- 1/4 teaspoon red pepper flakes
- 6 cups water (could substitute with low-sodium chicken broth)
- 1 1/4 pounds golden Yukon potatoes, peeled and cubed
- 2 bay leaves
- Pinch of salt
- Freshly ground black pepper, to taste

Directions:

1. In a large pot, heat olive oil over medium heat.
2. Add leeks, and sauté for 5-6 minutes, until leeks are soft and wilted.
3. Add thyme and red pepper, stir.
4. Add water, potatoes, and bay leaf. Bring to boil. Cover, reduce heat to low, and simmer until potatoes are tender, about 20 minutes.
5. Remove bay leaves and discard. Season with a pinch of salt and black pepper.
6. Using an immersion blender, puree soup until desired consistency. May also be blended, in 2-cup batches, in blender.

Nutritional Information (per serving)
- Calories: 150
- Sodium: 160 mg
- Protein: 9 g
- Carbs: 24 g
- Fat: 6 g

Easy Kale and White Bean Soup

*Canned soup is notoriously high in sodium. This low-sodium soup
can be prepared in just 30 minutes.*

Servings: 8

Ingredients:

- 2 tablespoons extra-virgin olive oil
- 1 medium yellow onion, diced
- 2 medium carrots, diced
- 2 celery stalks, diced
- 3 garlic cloves, minced
- 1/2 teaspoon red pepper flakes
- 1 tablespoon rosemary
- 6 cups low-sodium chicken broth
- 2 (15-ounce cans) white beans with liquid (buy the low-sodium version)
- 2 bay leaves
- 2 cups kale, chopped
- Freshly ground black pepper, to taste
- Parmesan cheese, grated, for serving

Directions:

1. In a large saucepan, heat olive oil over medium-high heat. Add onions, carrots, celery, and garlic, and cook, stirring frequently, for 3-4 minutes until softened.
2. Add red pepper flakes, rosemary, chicken broth, beans, and bay leaves. Turn heat to high and bring to a boil. Reduce heat to lowest setting, add kale, and simmer for 15 minutes.
3. Remove bay leaves and discard. Transfer two cups of soup to a blender and process until smooth. Return to pan and stir. (Alternatively, use immersion blender to puree soup to desired consistency.)
4. Season with ground black pepper and Parmesan cheese.

Nutritional Information (per serving)
- Calories: 260
- Sodium: 420 mg
- Protein: 26 g
- Carbs: 70 g
- Fat: 5 g

Curried Lentil Soup

This soup is full of both flavor and veggies.

Servings: 6

Ingredients:

- 2 tablespoons olive oil
- 1 medium onion, diced
- 1 large carrot, diced
- 1 celery stalk, diced
- 3 cloves garlic, minced
- 2 tablespoons curry powder
- 6 cups low-sodium chicken or vegetable broth
- 1 1/2 cups dried lentils, washed
- 1/2 teaspoon salt
- Freshly ground black pepper, to taste
- 1 can (13.5 ounces) coconut milk

Directions:

1. In a large pot, heat oil over medium heat. Add onion, carrot, celery, and garlic and sauté, stirring often, until softened, about 5-6 minutes. Add curry powder and stir for an additional minute.

2. Add in broth, lentils, salt and pepper. Stir, and bring to a boil over high heat. Cover, reduce heat to medium-low, and simmer until lentils are soft (35-40 minutes).

3. Using an immersion blender, puree soup to desired consistency. Stir in coconut milk. Heat gently over medium-low heat until heated through.

Nutritional Information (per serving)
- Calories: 400
- Sodium: 300 mg
- Protein: 19 g
- Carbs: 39 g
- Fat: 20 g

Greek Lemon-Drop Soup (Avgolemono)

Servings: 6

Ingredients:

- 6 cups low-sodium chicken broth
- 3/4 cup long-grain rice
- 3 chicken breast halves, skinless, cooked and shredded
- 2 eggs
- 1/3 cup lemon juice
- Lemon slices, for garnish

Directions:

1. In a large saucepan, bring chicken broth and rice to a boil. Reduce heat, cover, and simmer for 15 minutes. Add chicken and simmer for an additional 2-3 minutes. Remove from heat.
2. In a bowl, whisk together eggs and lemon juice. Slowly add in 1 cup of hot soup broth, whisking continuously. Add warm egg mixture to soup pot and mix to combine.
3. Serve with a slice of lemon.

Nutritional Information (per serving)
- Calories: 315
- Sodium: 180 mg
- Protein: 28 g
- Carbs: 36 g
- Fat: 7 g

Apple, Blue Cheese, and Pistachio Salad

The slightly sweet apples, savory cheese, and crunchy pistachios make for a welcome contrast of flavors.

Servings: 4

Ingredients:

- 3 apples, peeled, cored, and cubed
- 1 tablespoon lemon juice
- 1 cup plain lowfat or nonfat yogurt, preferable Greek-style
- 1/4 teaspoon cayenne pepper
- 1/2 teaspoon black pepper
- 1/3 cup blue cheese, crumbled
- 1/3 cup pistachios

Directions:

1. Place apples in a bowl and sprinkle with lemon juice.
2. Add yogurt and pepper to apples and mix to combine. Place in refrigerator and chill for at least 30 minutes.
3. When ready to serve, add blue cheese and pistachios and mix well.

Nutritional Information (per serving)
- Calories: 200
- Sodium: 200 mg
- Protein: 8.5 g
- Carbs: 25 g
- Fat: 8.5 g

Warm Couscous Salad with Orange Vinaigrette

Couscous is a quick-cooking pasta made from semolina flour. It cooks in just 5 minutes for a delicious and quick meal.

Servings: 6

Ingredients:

- 1 1/2 cups low sodium chicken broth
- 2 tablespoons olive oil, divided
- 1/4 teaspoon salt
- 1 box couscous (1 1/2 cups)
- 1/4 cup orange juice
- 2 tablespoons white wine vinegar
- Freshly ground black pepper
- 3 scallions, finely chopped
- 2 tablespoons fresh flat-leaf parsley, chopped
- 1/3 cup sliced almonds

Directions:

1. In a medium-size pot, add chicken broth, and 1 tablespoon olive oil. Bring to boil. Add couscous, stir, and cover. Remove from heat and let sit for 5 minutes. Fluff with fork.
2. While couscous sits, whisk together remaining tablespoon olive oil, orange juice, vinegar, 1/4 teaspoon salt, and black pepper in a bowl.
3. Pour vinaigrette over couscous and stir well to combine. Add in scallions, herbs, and sliced almonds. Season with additional ground pepper.
4. Serve warm.

Nutritional Information (per serving)
- Calories: 375
- Sodium: 230 mg
- Protein: 9 g
- Carbs: 52 g
- Fat: 15 g

Arugula Salad with Orange, Beets, and Feta

This salad has a sweet, refreshing taste and is full of antioxidants.

Servings: 4

Ingredients:

- 2 medium beets
- 2 naval oranges
- 2 tablespoons orange juice
- 1 1/2 tablespoons extra-virgin olive oil
- 1 tablespoon balsamic vinegar
- Pinch of salt
- Pinch of black pepper
- 2 cups baby arugula
- 1/4 cup feta cheese, crumbled
- 1 tablespoon sunflower seeds, roasted and unsalted

Directions:

1. Peel beets and place in saucepan. Cover with water and bring to boil over high heat. Reduce heat and simmer until tender, about 15 minutes. Drain and set aside to cool.
2. Peel oranges and cut into sections.
3. Make dressing by whisking together orange juice, olive oil, balsamic vinegar, salt, and pepper.
4. To assemble salad, divide arugula evenly between 4 bowls. Top with beets and orange sections. Drizzle with salad dressing. Sprinkle with feta cheese and sunflower seeds.

Nutritional Information (per serving)
- Calories: 165
- Sodium: 90 mg
- Protein: 5 g
- Carbs: 15 g
- Fat: 8 g

California Cobb Salad

This hearty salad makes a complete lunch or dinner.

Servings: 4

Ingredients:

- 10 ounces baby spinach
- 2 tablespoons extra-virgin olive oil
- 1 1/2 tablespoons lemon juice
- 3 slices low-sodium bacon, cooked
- 2 large eggs, hard-boiled, shells removed, cut into bite-sized pieces
- 2 cups cooked chicken, skinless, cut into bite-sized pieces
- 1 cup grape tomatoes, halved
- 2 avocadoes, pitted, cut into bit-sized pieces
- 1/3 cup blue cheese, crumbled
- Freshly ground black pepper, to taste

Directions:

1. In a large bowl, toss spinach with olive oil and lemon juice.
2. Add bacon, eggs, chicken, tomatoes, avocado, and blue cheese. Toss to combine. Season with pepper to taste.

Nutritional Information (per serving)
- Calories: 450
- Sodium: 450 mg
- Protein: 25 g
- Carbs: 15 g
- Fat: 34 g

Southwest Corn and Black Bean Salad

This easy-to-make salad is a perfect accompaniment to grilled chicken or beef.

Servings: 12

Ingredients:

- 1 (15.5 ounce) can black beans, low-sodium, rinsed and drained
- 1 cup cooked corn, fresh or frozen
- 1/2 medium red onion, chopped
- 1 medium tomato, chopped
- 1/2 cucumber, peeled and chopped
- 2 tablespoons fresh cilantro, minced
- 2 limes, juice of
- 1 tablespoon extra-virgin olive oil
- 1 medium avocado, pitted and diced
- Freshly ground black pepper, to taste

Directions:

1. Combine beans, corn, onions, tomato, cucumber, and cilantro into large bowl. Sprinkle with lime juice and toss to combine. Pour on olive oil and mix again.
2. Let marinate in refrigerator for at least 30 minutes.
3. Before serving, add avocado and season with pepper to taste.

Nutritional Information (per serving)
- Calories: 85
- Sodium: 138 mg
- Protein: 4 g
- Carbs: 13 g
- Fat: 5 g

Curried Chicken Salad

*This can be served on top of a bed of greens or made into a sandwich
by using in a whole-wheat pita.*

Servings: 4

Ingredients:

- 1/2 cup nonfat plain yogurt, Greek style
- 1 tablespoon curry powder
- 2 cups cooked chicken, skinless, cut into bite-size pieces
- 1 medium apple, peeled and diced
- 1 stalk celery, diced
- 1/2 cup dried cranberries
- 1/4 cup sesame seeds, roasted and unsalted

Directions:

1. Combine yogurt and curry powder in a bowl. Add chicken, apple, celery, cranberries, and sesame seeds. Toss to combine.
2. Can be made ahead and stored in the refrigerator for up to 2 days.

Nutritional Information (per serving)
- Calories: 259
- Sodium: 230 mg
- Protein: 24 g
- Carbs: 27 g
- Fat: 6 g

MAIN DISHES

Chicken Alfredo with Whole-Wheat Bowtie Pasta

Servings: 6

Ingredients:

- 12 ounces whole wheat bowtie pasta
- 2 tablespoons olive oil
- 3 chicken breasts, boneless and skinless
- 2 cloves garlic
- 3/4 low-sodium chicken broth
- 1/2 cup half-and-half
- 3/4 cup grated Parmesan cheese
- 2 tablespoons fresh parsley, minced
- Freshly ground black pepper, to taste

Directions:

1. Cook pasta according to package directions. Drain and set aside.
2. In a large skillet, heat 2 tablespoons of olive oil over medium-high heat. Add chicken breasts and cook until golden brown and done in the middle, about 5-6 minutes per side. Remove from pan, slice into bite-size pieces, set aside.
3. Add remaining 2 tablespoons of olive oil to pan. Add garlic and sauté for 1 minute. Pour in broth and let it boil for about 2 minutes. Add half-and-half and whisk together. Continuing cooking, stirring frequently, for several minutes until liquid starts to thicken.
4. Remove pan from and add Parmesan cheese, chicken, and pasta. Season with black pepper. Toss all ingredients together until well combined. If sauce is too thick, add a little extra chicken broth to thin it down.
5. Serve topped with parsley and additional Parmesan cheese, if desired.

Nutritional Information (per serving)
- Calories: 490
- Sodium: 450 mg
- Protein: 28 g
- Carbs: 46 g
- Fat: 19 g

Simple Baked Chicken

This is a simple, classic dish.

Servings: 4

Ingredients:

- 3-4 pound chicken, cut into parts
- 2-3 tablespoons olive oil
- 1/2 teaspoon thyme
- 1/4 teaspoon sea salt
- Freshly ground black pepper
- 1/2 cup low-sodium chicken stock

Directions:

1. Preheat oven to 400 degrees F.
2. Trim off any excess fat from chicken pieces. Rinse and pat dry with paper towels.
3. Rub olive oil over chicken pieces. Sprinkle with thyme, salt, and pepper.
4. Arrange chicken pieces in roasting pan.
5. Bake chicken in oven for 30 minutes. Lower heat to 350 degrees F and bake for an addition 15-30 minutes, or until juice run clear.
6. Remove from oven. Let rest for 5 to 10 minutes before serving.

Nutritional Information (per serving)
- Calories: 550
- Sodium: 480 mg
- Protein: 91 g
- Carbs: 0 g
- Fat: 19 g

Orange Chicken and Broccoli Stir Fry

Skip the Chinese takeout and serve this delicious healthy stir fry instead.

Servings: 4

Ingredients:

- 1 tablespoon olive oil or coconut oil
- 1 pound chicken breast, boneless and skinless, cut into strips
- 1/3 cup orange juice
- 2 tablespoons low-sodium soy sauce
- 2 teaspoons cornstarch
- 2 cups broccoli, cut into small pieces
- 1 cup snow peas
- 2 cups cabbage, shredded
- 2 cups brown rice, cooked
- 1 tablespoon sesame seeds (optional)

Directions:

1. In a bowl, combine orange juice, soy sauce, and corn starch. Set aside.
2. Heat oil in wok or large sauté pan. Add chicken and stir fry for 4-5 minutes or until chicken is golden brown on all sides.
3. Add broccoli, snow peas, cabbage, and sauce mixture. Continue to stir fry until vegetables are tender but still crisp, about 7-8 minutes.
4. Serve over brown rice and sprinkle with sesame seeds.

Nutritional Information (per serving)
- Calories: 340
- Sodium: 240 mg
- Protein: 28 g
- Carbs: 35 g
- Fat: 8 g

Mediterranean Lemon Chicken and Potatoes

Servings: 4
Ingredients:

- 1 1/2 pounds chicken breast, skinless and boneless, cut into 1-inch cubes
- 1 pound Yukon Gold potatoes, cut into cubes
- 1 medium onion, chopped
- 1 red or yellow pepper, chopped
- 1/2 cup low-sodium vinaigrette
- 1/4 cup lemon juice
- 1 teaspoon oregano
- 1/2 teaspoon garlic powder
- 1/2 cup chopped tomato
- Freshly ground black pepper, to taste

Directions:

1. Mix all ingredients except tomatoes together in large bowl.
2. Lay out 4 large squares of aluminum foil. Place equal amount of chicken and potato mixture in the center of each square. Fold top and sides to enclose mixture in packet.
3. Bake in preheated 400 degree F oven for 30 minutes or until chicken and potatoes are cooked through. Packet may also be cooked on the grill.
4. Open packets and top with chopped tomatoes. Season with black pepper to taste.

Nutritional Information (per serving)
- Calories: 320
- Sodium: 420 mg
- Protein: 43 g
- Carbs: 34 g
- Fat: 4 g

Tandoori Chicken

This chicken dish is packed with flavor. You can adjust the amount of spiciness you want by adding or reducing the amount of red pepper flakes.

Servings: 6

Ingredients:

- 1 cup nonfat yogurt, plain
- 1/2 cup lemon juice
- 5 garlic cloves, crushed
- 2 tablespoons paprika
- 1 teaspoon curry powder
- 1 teaspoon ground ginger
- 1 teaspoon red pepper flakes
- 6 chicken breasts, skinless and boneless, cut into 2-inch chunks
- 6 skewers (soaked in water if using wooden skewers)

Directions:

1. Preheat oven to 400 degrees F.
2. In a bowl, combine yogurt, lemon juice, garlic, and spices. Blend well.
3. Divide chicken evenly and thread onto skewers. Place skewers in shallow baking or casserole dish. Pour half of yogurt mixture onto chicken. Cover and refrigerate for 15-20 minutes.
4. Spray another baking dish with nonstick cooking spray. Place chicken skewers in pan. Coat with remaining 1/2 of yogurt marinade.
5. Bake in oven for 15-20 minutes or until chicken is cooked through and juices run clear. Alternatively, chicken can cooked on a grill.

Note: Serve over brown rice with steamed veggies on the side.

Nutritional Information (per serving)
- Calories: 175
- Sodium: 105 mg
- Protein: 30 g
- Carbs: 8 g
- Fat: 2 g

Steak Smothered in Mushrooms

Sirloin steak topped with mushrooms in a balsamic sauce.

Servings: 4

Ingredients:

- 1 pound sirloin steak
- 1 tablespoon olive oil
- 1 1/2 cups mushrooms, sliced
- 2 tablespoons butter
- 1/2 tablespoon all-purpose flour
- Freshly ground black pepper, to taste
- 3 tablespoons balsamic vinegar

Directions:

1. Heat oil in large nonstick skillet over medium-high heat. Add steak and cook, turning once, until desired doneness. Remove steak from pan and slice into thin strips.
2. In same skillet, add mushrooms and butter. Sprinkle with flour and continue cooking, stirring occasionally, until mushrooms start to brown. About 5-6 minutes. Season with black pepper.
3. Add in vinegar and cook for an additional 2 minutes, stir ring frequently.
4. Serve steak with mushroom mixture on top.

Nutritional Information (per serving)
- Calories: 175
- Sodium: 105 mg
- Protein: 30 g
- Carbs: 8 g
- Fat: 2 g

Slow-Cooker Beef Stew Provencal

Servings: 10

Ingredients:

Bouquet garni

- Cheesecloth
- 1 bay leaf
- 1 stalk celery, chopped
- 3 sprigs fresh parsley
- 3 sprigs fresh thyme

Stew

- 2 tablespoons extra-virgin olive oil, divided
- 3 pounds beef chuck (or other stew meat), cut into 1-inch pieces
- 2 teaspoons kosher salt, divided
- 1/2 teaspoon freshly ground pepper, divided
- 2 medium yellow onions, chopped
- 4 cloves garlic, minced
- 3-4 large carrots, sliced into 1-inch rounds
- 2 tablespoons tomato paste, no salt added
- 1 pound mushrooms, sliced
- 1 quart beef stock, low-sodium
- 1/4 cup red wine

Directions:

1. To assemble bouquet garni, cut a square of cheesecloth. Place bay leaf, celery, parsley, and thyme in center. Tie with kitchen twine.
2. To prepare stew heat 1 tablespoon olive oil in large heavy-duty pan. Add beef cubes and until browned on all sides. Transfer to slow cooker, season with 1 teaspoon salt and black pepper.
3. Add another tablespoon of oil to pan and add onions, garlic, and carrots. Cook, stirring occasionally until they begin to soften, about 4-5 minutes. Season with remaining salt and pepper. Add to slow cooker with beef.
4. Add tomato paste, mushrooms, beef stock, red wine, and bouquet garni to slow cooker. Stir to combine.
5. Cover and cook on low setting for 8-9 hours or high setting for 5-6 hours.

Nutritional Information (per serving)
• Calories: 351
• Sodium: 380 mg
• Protein: 26 g
• Carbs: 14 g
• Fat: 15 g

Slow-Cooker Turkey Stroganoff

Servings: 6

Ingredients:

- 4 cups mushrooms, sliced (can use a mix of types)
- 3 medium carrots, sliced into 1-inch rounds
- 1 small onion, chopped fine
- One 3-4 pound split turkey breast, skin removed (can substitute with chicken breast)
- 1/3 cup all-purpose flour
- 1 cup nonfat Greek-style plain yogurt
- 1 tablespoon lemon juice
- 1/4 dry sherry (not cooking sherry)
- 1 cup frozen peas, thawed
- Freshly ground black pepper, to taste
- 12 ounces whole-wheat egg noodles, cooked
- 1/4 cup flat-leaf parsley, chopped

Directions:

1. Place mushrooms, carrots, onion, and turkey in a 5-6 quart slow cooker. Cover and cook on low for 8 hours or on high for 4 hours.
2. Remove turkey and place on cutting board.
3. In a bowl, whisk together flour, yogurt, lemon juice, and sherry. Add to slow cooker along with peas and pepper. Stir, cover, and cook on high for about 15 minutes.
4. Remove turkey meat from bone and cut into bite-size pieces. Place turkey pieces back in slow cooker and stir.
5. Serve over egg noodles and top with chopped parsley.

Nutritional Information (per serving)
- Calories: 440
- Sodium: 480 mg
- Protein: 46 g
- Carbs: 43 g
- Fat: 6 g

Panko-Crusted Cod

Panko are Japanese style breadcrumbs and provide a crunchy taste. Available in most supermarkets.

Servings: 2

Ingredients:

- 1/4 Panko-style breadcrumbs
- 1 clove garlic, minced
- 1 tablespoon extra-virgin olive oil
- 3 tablespoons nonfat Greek yogurt
- 1 tablespoon mayonnaise
- 1 1/2 teaspoons lemon juice
- 1/2 teaspoon tarragon
- Pinch of salt
- 10 ounces cod, cut into two portions

Directions:

1. Preheat oven to 425 degrees F. Coat baking pan with non-stick cooking spray.
2. In a small bowl, combine breadcrumbs, garlic and olive oil.
3. In another bowl, combine yogurt, mayonnaise, lemon juice, tarragon, and salt.
4. Place fish in baking pan. Top each piece with one half yogurt mixture and then 1/3 breadcrumb mixture.
5. Bake in oven for 15 minutes or until fish is opaque in center and breadcrumbs are golden brown.

Nutritional Information (per serving)
- Calories: 225
- Sodium: 270 mg
- Protein: 18 g
- Carbs: 13 g
- Fat: 10 g

Grilled Salmon and Asparagus with Lemon Butter

Salmon is rich in heart-healthy omega-3s. Buy wild salmon whenever possible.

Servings: 4

Ingredients:

- 1 1/4 pounds salmon, cut into 4 portions
- 2 bunches asparagus, ends trimmed
- Cooking spray, preferably olive oil
- 1/2 teaspoon salt
- 1/4 teaspoon freshly ground pepper
- 1/4 teaspoon garlic powder
- 1 tablespoon olive oil
- 1 tablespoon butter
- 3 tablespoons lemon juice

Directions:

1. Place salmon and asparagus on large rimmed baking sheet. Spray lightly with cooking spray. Sprinkle with salt, pepper, and garlic powder.
2. Place asparagus and salmon on preheated, oiled grill. Grill the salmon, turning once, until opaque, about 3-5 minutes per side. Grill the asparagus, turning occasionally, until tender, about 5-7 minutes.
3. In a microwave-safe bowl, place olive oil, butter, and lemon juice. Microwave to melt butter, about 20 seconds. Drizzle fish with butter-lemon mixture. Serve immediately.

Note: This can also be cooked under the broiler instead of the grill.

Nutritional Information (per serving)
- Calories: 190
- Sodium: 445 mg
- Protein: 24 g
- Carbs: 6 g
- Fat: 8 g

61

Oven-Barbecued Pork Chops

When it's too cold outside for the grill, cook these up for an indoor barbecue.

Servings: 4

Ingredients:

- 4 bone-in 3/4-inch thick pork chops (about 1 1/2 pounds)
- 1/4 teaspoon salt
- 1/4 teaspoon freshly ground black pepper
- 1 tablespoon plus 1 teaspoon olive oil
- 1 medium onion , diced
- 3 cloves garlic, minced
- 1/3 cup orange juice
- 1/2 cup low-sodium barbecue sauce

Directions:

1. Preheat oven to 400 degrees F.
2. Heat 1 tablespoon olive oil in ovenproof skillet over high heat. Add pork chops, season with salt and pepper, and cook until browned, 1 to 2 minutes per side. Transfer to plate.
3. Add remaining 1 teaspoon olive oil to pan. Add onion and garlic and cook, stirring, until softened, 3-4 minutes. Add orange juice and continue cooking until most of liquid is evaporated, 2-3 minutes. Add in barbecue sauce, stir.
4. Return pork chops to pan, turning to coat with sauce.
5. Transfer pan to oven and bake until pork chops are cooked (internal temperature of 145 F), about 7-8 minutes.
6. Serve pork chops topped with sauce.

Nutritional Information (per serving)
- Calories: 245
- Sodium: 390 mg
- Protein: 20 g
- Carbs: 15 g
- Fat: 10 g

Whole-Wheat Spaghetti with Ragu Sauce

Store-bought spaghetti sauce is full of sodium. Try this easy, home-made version instead for a healthy meal.

Servings: 8
Ingredients:

- 1 box whole-wheat spaghetti
- 1 tablespoon extra-virgin olive oil
- 1 medium onion, chopped fine
- 1 large carrot, chopped fine
- 1 stalk celery, chopped fine
- 4 cloves garlic, minced
- 1 teaspoon oregano
- 1 teaspoon basil
- 1 teaspoon marjoram
- 1 pound lean ground beef
- 1 28-ounce can crushed tomatoes, no salt added
- 1/2 teaspoon salt
- 1/4 cup flat-leaf parsley, chopped
- 1/2 cup grated Parmesan cheese

Directions:

1. Cook spaghetti according to package directions. Drain.
2. While pasta cooks, heat oil in large skillet over medium heat. Add onion, carrot, and celery and cooking, stirring oc casionally, until onion turns translucent, about 5 minutes. Add in garlic and seasonings, and cook for another 30 seconds.
3. Add beef and cook, stirring, until meat is browned and no longer pink, about 4-5 minutes. Add crushed toma toes and continue to cook, stirring occasionally, until sauce thickens, about 5 minutes. Season with salt and add parsley.
4. To serve, plate 1 cup of pasta, top with sauce and sprinkle with Parmesan cheese.

Note: Sauce can be made ahead and kept in the refrigerator for up to 3 days.

Nutritional Information (per serving)
- Calories: 385
- Sodium: 415 mg
- Protein: 28 g
- Carbs: 52 g
- Fat: 9 g

Sausage and Chicken Stew

This hearty stew can be served over whole-wheat pasta or brown rice.
Servings: 8
Ingredients:

- 1 tablespoon extra-virgin olive oil
- 8 ounces chorizo sausage, diced
- 2 medium yellow onions, chopped
- 3 cloves garlic, minced
- 3 pounds chicken thighs, boneless and skinless, cut into 1-inch pieces
- 2 tablespoons paprika
- 1/2 teaspoon sea salt
- Freshly ground black pepper, to taste
- 3 cups white wine
- 2 14.5 ounce cans diced tomatoes, no salt added
- 2 cups low-sodium chicken broth
- 1/4 cup flat-leaf parsley, chopped
- 1 pinch saffron

Directions:

1. In a large pot or Dutch oven, heat oil over medium heat. Add sausage and cook, stirring occasionally, for 6-7 minutes. Add onion and garlic, and continue to cook, stirring occasionally for 8-10 minutes, until onion is soft.
2. Add chicken, paprika, salt, and pepper, stir to coat. Cook for another 5 minutes, stirring occasionally.
3. Add wine, turn heat to high and cook until wine is reduced by a third, about 7-8 minutes.
4. Add tomatoes, chicken broth, parsley, and saffron. Reduce heat to low and simmer, uncovered, until sauce has thickened and chicken is tender, about 1 hour.
5. Season with additional pepper, to taste.

Nutritional Information (per serving)
- Calories: 185
- Sodium: 230 mg
- Protein: 16 g
- Carbs: 7 g
- Fat: 7 g

Pasta Primavera with Shrimp and Spinach Fettuccine

Packed with veggies, this meal is tasty and quick.

Servings: 6

Ingredients:

- 1/2 pound fresh asparagus, trimmed, cut into 1-inch lengths
- 12 ounces spinach fettuccine (can substitute whole-wheat if desired)
- 2 teaspoons olive oil
- 3 garlic cloves, minced
- 1/4 teaspoon crushed red pepper
- 1 pound medium shrimp, peeled and deveined (thawed if frozen)
- 1 cup green peas, fresh or frozen
- 1/2 cup green onion, sliced thin
- 1 tablespoon lemon juice
- 1 tablespoon fresh parsley, chopped
- 1/3 cup Parmesan cheese, grated
- 1/2 teaspoon salt
- Freshly ground black pepper, to taste

Directions:

1. Fill a large pot with water and bring to a boil. Add asparagus and cook until tender but still crisp, about 4 minutes. Remove from water with slotted spoon and set aside. Add pasta to water and cooking according to package directions. Set aside.
2. In a large skillet, heat olive oil over medium heat. Add garlic and crushed red pepper and cook, stirring, for about a minute. Add shrimp, peas, and green onion and cook, stirring, for 3-4 minutes.
3. Add reserved pasta and asparagus along with lemon juice, parsley, and Parmesan cheese. Season with salt and pepper. Toss to coat.
4. Serve hot.

Nutritional Information (per serving)
• Calories: 360
• Sodium: 380 mg
• Protein: 26 g
• Carbs: 49 g
• Fat: 6 g

Quick and Easy Chili

Great-tasting, this chili can be prepared with just a few ingredients.

Servings: 6

Ingredients:

- 1/2 pound lean ground beef
- 1/2 medium yellow onion, diced
- 1 can (15.5) low-sodium kidney beans, drained
- 1 can (14.5 ounces) diced tomatoes
- 1 1/2 tablespoons chili powder

Directions:

1. In a large skillet brown ground meat and onions over medium-high heat (about 6-7 minutes). Drain excess fat.
2. Add beans, tomatoes, and chili powder.
3. Reduce heat to low, cover, and simmer for 10 minutes.
4. Serve with brown rice.

Nutritional Information (per serving)
- Calories: 220
- Sodium: 430 mg
- Protein: 16 g
- Carbs: 21 g
- Fat: 7 g

Pork Tenderloin with Apples and Sweet Potatoes

This one-pot meal includes servings of fruit, vegetables, and lean meat.

Servings: 4

Ingredients:

- 3/4 cup apple cider
- 1/4 cup apple cider vinegar
- 3 tablespoons maple syrup
- 1/2 teaspoon paprika
- 1 teaspoon fresh grated ginger (or 1/4 teaspoon dried)
- 1 teaspoon ground black pepper
- 2 teaspoons olive oil
- 1 12-ounce pork tenderloin
- 1 large sweet potato, peeled, cut into small cubes
- 1 large apple, peeled, cut into small cubes

Directions:

1. Preheat oven to 375 degrees F.
2. In a bowl, combine apple cider, vinegar, maple syrup, paprika, ginger, and pepper.
3. In a Dutch oven or large ovenproof sauté pan, heat oil over medium heat. Add pork tenderloin and cook, turning, until all sides are browned, about 8-10 minutes. Remove pan from heat.
4. Add sweet potatoes to pan around the pork. Pour apple cider mixture over pork. Cover and bake in oven for 20 minutes or until tenderloin reaches internal temperature of 145-150 degrees F.
5. Remove pan from oven and add apple pieces. Return to oven and cook, uncovered, for another 8-10 minutes, or until tenderloin reaches 170 degrees.
6. Let sit for 10 minutes before slicing pork.
7. Serve pork with apples and sweet potatoes on side. Cover with any remaining sauce.

Nutritional Information (per serving)
- Calories: 280
- Sodium: 240 mg
- Protein: 20 g
- Carbs: 40 g
- Fat: 5 g

Lemon-Orange Orange Roughy

Light and citrusy and cooks up very quickly.

Servings: 4

Ingredients:

- 1 tablespoon olive oil
- 4 (4 ounce) fillets of orange roughy
- Juice of 1 orange
- Juice of 1 lemon
- 1/2 teaspoon black pepper

Directions:

1. Heat oil in a large skillet over medium-high heat. Place fillet in skillet and drizzle with orange and lemon juice. Sprinkle with black pepper.
2. Cover and cook for 5-6 minutes or until fish flakes easily with fork.

Note: Orange roughy can be substituted with any firm mild fish such as flounder, sole, haddock, or tilapia.

Nutritional Information (per serving)
- Calories: 140
- Sodium: 140 mg
- Protein: 19 g
- Carbs: 8 g
- Fat: 4 g

Steak Tacos

Authentic-style Mexican tacos.

Servings: 6
Ingredients:

- 1 1/4 pounds sirloin steak, cut into strips
- 1/4 teaspoon salt
- Freshly ground black pepper, to taste
- 2 tablespoons plus 2 teaspoons olive oil
- 12 (6-inch) tortillas
- 1/2 red onion, diced
- 3 fresh jalapeno peppers, seeded and chopped
- 1/2 bunch fresh cilantro, chopped
- 3 limes, cut into wedges

Directions:

1. In a large skillet, heat 2 tablespoons olive oil over medium-high heat. Add steak and sauté until browned on all sides and cooked through to desired doneness, about 5-6 minutes. Season with salt and pepper. Remove from pan to plate and cover to keep warm.
2. In same skillet, add 2 more teaspoons olive oil and allow to get hot. Add tortillas, one at a time, and cook turning once, until tortilla is lightly browned but still flexible.
3. To assemble tacos, place tortilla on a plate and top with steak, onion, jalapeno peppers, and cilantro. Squeeze lime juice over top.

Nutritional Information (per serving)
- Calories: 380
- Sodium: 115 mg
- Protein: 20 g
- Carbs: 28 g
- Fat: 21 g

SNACKS, SIDES, AND DESSERTS

Caramelized Onions and Bell Peppers

This makes a great side dish to pork or beef dishes.

Servings: 4

Ingredients:

- 2 red bell peppers, cut into strips
- 2 red onions, sliced thin
- 1 tablespoon olive oil
- 1 teaspoon butter, unsalted
- 1/4 red wine
- Pinch of salt
- Freshly ground black pepper, to taste
- 1/4 teaspoon dried basil

Directions:

1. Heat oil and butter in skillet over medium heat. Add peppers and onion and sauté, stirring, for 2 minutes. Reduce heat to medium-low and continue to cook until onions and peppers soften, about 4-5 minutes.

2. Add red wine and continue to cook until wine has reduced by half, about 15-20 minutes. Season with salt, pepper, and basil.

Nutritional Information (per serving)
- Calories: 95
- Sodium: 110 mg
- Protein: 9 g
- Carbs: 9.5 g
- Fat: 5 g

Sweet Potato Casserole

A crunchy pecan topping makes this feel like a decadent treat.

Servings: 8

Ingredients:

- 2 1/4 cups sweet potatoes, peeled, cooked, and mashed
- 1/4 cup butter, melted
- 2 tablespoons low-fat milk
- 1/4 cup honey
- 1/4 teaspoon vanilla
- 1 egg, beaten
- 1/4 cup brown sugar
- 1/4 cup all-purpose flour
- 3 tablespoons butter
- 1/2 cup chopped pecans

Directions:

1. Preheat oven to 350 degrees F. Spray a 8 x 11 inch baking pan with cooking spray
2. In a large bowl, mix together sweet potatoes, melted butter, milk, honey, vanilla, and egg.
3. In a small bowl, mix together brown sugar and flour. Cut in 3 tablespoons butter until mixture is crumbly. Add pecans and stir.
4. Sprinkle pecan mixture over sweet potatoes.
5. Bank in oven for 25 minutes or until golden brown.

Nutritional Information (per serving)
- Calories: 310
- Sodium: 105 mg
- Protein: 3.2 g
- Carbs: 36 g
- Fat: 13 g

Kale Chips

Next time you are craving potato chips, reach for these low-cal snacks instead.

Servings: 6
Ingredients:
- 1 large bunch kale
- 1 tablespoon olive oil
- 1/4 teaspoon sea salt

Directions
1. Preheat oven to 350 degrees. Line cookie sheet with parchment paper.
2. Cut stems from kale. Wash and thoroughly dry kale leaves.
3. Spread kale out on baking sheet in single layer. Drizzle with olive oil and season with salt.
4. Bake until edges are browned, about 10-12 minutes.

Nutritional Information (per serving)
- Calories: 110
- Sodium: 210 mg
- Protein: 5 g
- Carbs: 16 g
- Fat: 5 g

Blueberry Sorbet

Sorbet is a refreshing way to satisfy a sweet tooth.

Servings: 8 (1/2 cup each)

Ingredients:

- 4 cups frozen blueberries
- 1 cup water
- 2-4 tablespoons confectioners' sugar or superfine sugar

Directions:

1. Place all ingredients in a blender and puree until smooth.
2. Strain through a fine sieve, pressing to extract as much of the liquid as possible. Discard solids.
3. Process mixture ice cream maker according to manufacturer's instructions.

Note: To make without ice cream maker, pour mixture into a baking pan and place in freezer. Every 30 minutes, stir with fork, moving frozen edges toward center. Repeat until firm and slushy, about 2 1/2 to 3 hours.

Nutritional Information (per serving)
- Calories: 46
- Sodium: 3 mg
- Protein: 1 g
- Carbs: 11 g
- Fat: 0 g

Microwave-Baked Stuffed Apples

Perfect for dessert on a crisp autumn day.

Servings: 4

Ingredients:

- 4 large apples
- 1/4 cup coconut flakes
- 1/4 cup dried cranberries or apricots
- 2 teaspoons orange zest, grated
- 1/2 cup orange juice
- 2 tablespoons brown sugar

Directions:

1. Cut top off apple and hollow out center with knife or apple corer. Arrange apples in a microwave-safe dish.
2. In a bowl, combine coconut, cranberries, and orange zest. Divide evenly and fill centers of apples.
3. In a bowl, mix orange juice and brown sugar. Pour over apples. Cover with microwave-safe plastic wrap and microwave on high for 7-8 minutes or until apples are tender.
4. Serve warm.

Nutritional Information (per serving)
- Calories: 190
- Sodium: 275 mg
- Protein: 1 g
- Carbs: 46 g
- Fat: 2 g

Carrot Cake Cookies

These cookies are full of carrot cake flavor in every bit.

Servings: 24 cookies

Ingredients

- 1/4 cup packed light-brown sugar
- 1/4 cup sugar
- 1/4 cup oil
- 1/4 cup applesauce or fruit puree
- 1 eggs
- 1/2 teaspoon vanilla
- 1/2 cup flour
- 1/2 cup whole wheat flour
- 1/2 teaspoon baking soda
- 1/2 teaspoon baking powder
- 1/8 teaspoon salt
- 1/2 teaspoon ground cinnamon
- 1/4 teaspoon ground nutmeg
- 1/4 teaspoon ground ginger
- 1 cups old-fashioned rolled oats (raw)
- 3/4 cup finely grated carrots (about 2 carrots)
- 1/2 cup raisins or golden raisins

Directions:

1. Preheat oven to 350 degrees F.
2. Mix together sugars, oil, applesauce, egg, and vanilla.
3. In a separate bowl, mix together all dry ingredients.
4. Add dry ingredients into wet ingredients. Mix until just blended. Stir in carrots and raisins.
5. Drop by teaspoonful on parchment-lined cookie sheet.
6. Bake 12-14 minutes or until golden brown.

Nutritional Information (per cookie)
- Calories: 80
- Sodium: 55 mg
- Protein: 1 g
- Carbs: 13 g
- Fat: 3 g

Oatmeal Walnut Chocolate Chip Cookies

We've reduced the amount of saturated fat in these cookies without sacrificing any of the taste.

Servings: 24 cookies

Ingredients:

- 1 cup rolled oats (not quick-cooking)
- 1/4 cup all-purpose flour
- 1/4 cup whole-wheat pastry flour
- 1/2 teaspoon ground cinnamon
- 1/4 teaspoon baking soda
- 1/4 teaspoon salt
- 1/4 cup tahini (sesame seed paste)
- 4 tablespoons cold unsalted butter, cut into pieces
- 1/3 cup granulated sugar
- 1/3 cup packed light brown sugar
- 1 large egg
- 1/2 tablespoon vanilla extract
- 1/2 cup semisweet or bittersweet chocolate chips
- 1/4 cup chopped walnuts

Directions:

1. Preheat oven to 350 degrees F. Line 2 cookie sheets with parchment paper.
2. Mix together oats, flour, cinnamon, baking soda, and salt in bowl.
3. In another large bowl, whisk together tahini, butter, sugar, brown sugar, egg, and vanilla until smooth.
4. Add in oat mixture and mix until just moistened.
5. Stir in chocolate chips and walnuts.
6. Place tablespoon-size portions of batter on cookie sheets, allowing space between.
7. Bake for about 14-16 minutes or until cookies are golden brown.

Note: Tahini can be substituted with almond butter or other nut butter.

Nutritional Information (per cookie)
- Calories: 110
- Sodium: 45 mg
- Protein: 2 g
- Carbs: 15 g
- Fat: 5 g

Cranberry-Raspberry Fruit Bars

These bars are sweet yet tart.

Servings: 18 bars
Ingredients:
  Crust
  • 1/2 cup chopped nuts (pecans, walnuts, or almonds work great), divided
  • 1/2 cup rolled oats, divided
  • 3/4 cup whole wheat pastry flour
  • 3/4 cup all-purpose flour
  • 1/2 cup sugar
  • 1/2 teaspoon salt
  • tablespoons butter, unsalted, cut into pieces
  • 1 egg
  • 2 tablespoons olive oil
  • 1 teaspoon vanilla extract
  Filling
  • 5 cups cranberries
  • 1/2 cup orange juice
  • 3/4 cup sugar
  • 1/4 cup cornstarch
  • 1 1/2 teaspoons orange zest
  • 1 cup raspberries
  • 1 teaspoon vanilla

Directions:
1.   Preheat oven to 400 degrees F. Coat 9 x 13-inch pan with cooking spray.
2.   To make crust, combine 1/4 nuts, 1/4 oats, flour, sugar, and salt in food processor. Process until nuts are finely ground. Add butter and process until combined.
3.   Whisk together egg, oil, and vanilla in bowl. Add mixture to food pro cessor and pulse for 30-45 seconds. Take out 1/2 cup of mixture and combine in bowl with remaining nuts and oats. Reserve for topping.
4.   To prepare filling, combine 1/2 of cranberries, orange juice, sugar, and cornstarch in a saucepan. Heat over medium heat, stirring frequently, until mixture has thickened, about 4-5 minutes. Add remaining cranberries, orange zest, raspberries and vanilla.
5.   Spread crust mixture evenly on bottom pan. Press firmly to form crust. Spread fruit filling on top of crust. Sprinkle with reserved nut topping.
6.   Bake for 15 minutes at 400 degrees. Reduce heat to 350 and continue baking until crust and topping are golden brown, about 25-30 minutes.
7.   Cool before cutting.

Nutritional Information (per serving)

  • Calories: 210   • Carbs: 30 g
  • Sodium: 70 mg   • Fat: 9 g
  • Protein: 3 g

Chocolate Surprise Brownies

The "surprise" in these brownies are the hidden vegetables – but you don't have to tell anyone!

Servings: 18 brownies

Ingredients:
- 1 cup black beans, low-sodium, rinsed and drained
- 2 tablespoons extra-virgin olive oil
- 1/4 cup applesauce
- 2 whole eggs
- 1 egg yolk
- 3/4 cup sugar
- 3 tablespoons cocoa powder
- 3 ounces bittersweet chocolate
- 2 tablespoons butter, unsalted
- 1/2 teaspoon salt
- 2 teaspoons vanilla extract
- 1/2 cup all-purpose flour
- 1/3 cup mini chocolate chips
- 1/3 cup chopped walnuts

Directions:
1. Preheat oven to 350 degrees F.
2. Add black beans, olive oil, spinach, applesauce, eggs, sugar, and cocoa into a food processor. Process until smooth.
3. Place bittersweet chocolate and butter into a microwave-safe dish and microwave for 30 seconds or until chocolate has melted. Let cool.
4. Add melted chocolate, salt, and vanilla extract to processor. Blend. Transfer mixture to bowl. Stir in flour, chocolate chips and walnuts.
5. Pour batter into 9 x 13-inch pan coated with nonstick cooking spray. Bake for 25-30 minutes.
6. Cool before cutting.

Nutritional Information (per cookie)
- Calories: 155
- Sodium: 95 mg
- Protein: 3 g
- Carbs: 20 g
- Fat: 8 g

All-Purpose Seasoning Mix

Use this in place of salt to add flavor to any dish.

Ingredients:

- 1 tablespoon garlic powder
- 1 1/2 teaspoons dried basil
- 1 1/2 teaspoons dried parsley
- 1 1/4 teaspoons dried savory
- 1 1/2 teaspoons ground thyme
- 1 teaspoon onion powder
- 1 teaspoon black pepper
- 1/4 teaspoon cayenne pepper

Directions:

1. Mix all ingredients together in a bowl. Store in sealed jar.

Cajun Seasoning

Ingredients:

- 2 tablespoons paprika
- 1 tablespoon garlic powder
- 1 tablespoon onion powder
- 2 teaspoons white pepper
- 2 teaspoons black pepper
- 1 teaspoon cayenne pepper
- 2 teaspoons thyme
- 1 teaspoon oregano

Directions:

1. Mix all ingredients together in a bowl. Store in sealed jar.

Taco Seasoning

Ingredients:

- 2 tablespoons chili powder
- 2 tablespoons cumin
- 2 tablespoons oregano
- 1/2 teaspoon onion powder
- 1/2 teaspoon cayenne pepper

Directions:

1. Mix all ingredients together in a bowl. Store in sealed jar.

Index

From the Author

I hope you enjoyed the *The DASH Diet Cookbook: Quick and Easy DASH Diet Recipes for Health and Weight Loss* and that it helps you create easy, healthy Paleo meals for you and your family to enjoy!

Please check out our other titles in the DASH Diet series:

- *DASH Diet for Weight Loss*
- *DASH Diet for Beginners*
- *DASH Diet Slow Cooker Recipes*

More Bestselling Titles from Dylanna Press

Mason Jar Meals by Dylanna Press

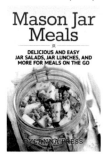

Mason jar meals are a fun and practical way to take your meals on the go. Mason jars are an easy way to prepare individual servings, so whether you're cooking for one, two, or a whole crowd, these fun, make-ahead meals will work.

Includes More than 50 Recipes and Full-Color Photos
In this book, you'll find a wide variety of recipes including all kinds of salads, as well as hot meal ideas such as mini chicken pot pies and lasagna in a jar. Also included are mouth-watering desserts such as strawberry shortcake, apple pie, and s'mores.

The recipes are easy to prepare and don't require any special cooking skills. So what are you waiting for? Grab your Mason jars and start preparing these gorgeous and tasty dishes!

The Inflammation Diet by Dylanna Press

Beat Pain, Slow Aging, and Reduce Risk of Heart Disease with the Inflammation Diet.

Inflammation has been called the "silent killer" and it has been linked to a wide variety of illnesses including heart disease, arthritis, diabetes, chronic pain, autoimmune disorders, and cancer.

Often, the root of chronic inflammation is in the foods we eat.

The Inflammation Diet: Complete Guide to Beating Pain and Inflammation will show you how, by making simple changes to your diet, you can greatly reduce inflammation in your body and reduce your symptoms and lower your risk of chronic disease.

The book includes a complete plan for eliminating inflammation and implementing an anti-inflammatory diet:

- Overview of inflammation and the body's immune response – what can trigger it and why chronic inflammation is harmful
- The link between diet and inflammation
- Inflammatory foods to avoid
- Anti-inflammatory foods to add to your diet to beat pain and inflammation
- Over 50 delicious inflammation diet recipes
- A 14-day meal plan

Take charge of your health and implement the inflammation diet to lose weight, slow the aging process, eliminate chronic pain, and reduce the likelihood and symptoms of chronic disease.

Learn how to heal your body from within through diet.

Made in the USA
San Bernardino, CA
14 February 2018